Susan Blanshard

Fragments Of The Human Heart

PAGE ADDIE PRESS UNITED KINGDOM AUSTRALIA

Contents

Mon Angel
Momento Fr. 1

Aotearoa is a savage place, seeding
A heap of broken images, mixing
Mortuary photographs with life
But this went further as
Milton sends an Angel
To whisper our chronicle
Opened-mouthed
At lip of headland
We passed the photo around
The world twice
Something you said
When I come back to you
Mon Angel never return
To this place.

Whose crayons, red and blue
Bruising each perfect soul
Until the color was evidence
Life has its way with us, against
Your body lover, we went down
Land falling from our skin
Sand falling from your hair
Passing the headland,
Aotearoa, your sky made me weep
Even as obscure, clouded places
A flap of wind, flax painted kite
Even as my breath catching, tearing
You away.

STANDING ON
THE FULL MOON

Which poet wrote graffiti in tombs.
All flesh is as grass. The voice said,
Cry. Then he asked: What shall I cry?
For the past, is a corpse
What does it mean
This dead and decaying thing
I want it back. I want to recover
What is found by another
The sound of saffron, mauve and gentian
Wakes you
With a shower of turquoise and indigo,
The miracle of all these waters

She is cool in the wetness of flesh
Opening and closing, the river, the lake
The moisture of all leaves
All her warm skin, keep touching.
It could still be felt
Against the grass
Only where you stand, keep standing.
After a while, the sound of
Someone cutting the lawn
The hard cracking in the garden of stones.
Summer day. The angel falls.
Broken off from yesterday.

J'Ai Plus De Souvenirs Que Si J'Avais Mille Ans

Counting the years lost
Like rings on a mango tree
I saw a blue tinge like a halo around these
Love letters, more passion,
Than microfilm could hold
Adulterate my thoughts, hide
More secrets, contains more sexual acts than
Your body could verify, where your hands
Touch, pale skin and silk,
Where musk, from the broken vial,
Breathe the perfume on a throat.

I am a room in a disused brothel
A red candle stolen from a church,
The edges of the atrium,
A wound, where
All love ends and begins again.
A stone jar of dreams, scar on a heart,
The face of a man, foreign postcard,
Souvenir maps, wrapped old feelings
I am the vault where this blueness stays,
The ink line of thread,
Embroiderer of parchment,
Inker of veins.

PABLO

For all this I asked you
by its promises of heat
between the rains
of you between
slats of moisture.
It wets my tongue like a
phallus, that cannot be tamed.

I had taken my place
above your open mouth
but what do you think,
to brand my lips so that I may
breathe close
instead of leaving you
there in the beginning. She would.

For the woman, is there but only
laid down, for the lover
as though
green grass has been planted
in an open field.
The morning when gentle color
Comes back as though
Nothing happened.

Momento Fr II

Closest to sleep and dreams,
the nearness of you
revival of musk & moss
moist color on the edges
and this instinct for kissing you.
Sweet exodus of perfume to open night.
In the secret excavation naked,
you make me forget there was ever a night
in which we were asleep.

FIRST OPERA OF WORDS
MOMENTO FR. III

It is a birth of dream, a child of our own
Possession
Everything, this sacrifice,
Not safe from your snares
And wires, in breach of the truth.

But who promises her bread, a crust
Cut from a thousand words
Whose ink in his hand, quenched truth?
Drown the dream carefully
Leave nothing , forget her
Bequeath her nothing
But one day she will be returned to you

In this month of erasure, she resembles you
She is wrapped in rags.
While rag world is her rag world
Yet perfumed cloth with oranges
But then oily stain of bitterest olives
Then who left to sweep up dead stones,
That penetrate white her bone
Hold her close, until rocks of her spine
Belong to your past
Let my name be traveler, first rains
And you shall be brought down,
And shall speak out of ground
A voice as low as dust
Shouts out of stone
We came to you for resurrection
When you needed complete obedience
The terrible repetitious history
In crush of law in the chain of time
We had nothing to obey.
I will find something in this stony rubbish,
The folded tent unbinding
(come inside and stay) and I will show you
What is left after losses, the remains of life,
We keep.

MATERNAL GHOST

She is lying there in the interval
waiting and even if I pressed the clover
or a flower between the book and
the room, air is measured
in lilac and violets
wind in the velvet,
smells of her perfume
the purple tracery on green stem
the web in narrow splinters.

She is bone and wool
treasure casket purple cloak
rag and calcified relic
of a resurrected saint
to hear your voice as solitary choir
to see your face smiling at the window
the halo. Highly glazed. It shines as if
I held a candle to it. Even the sound when
she dropped a coin in the box. Disappeared.
One does not imagine this.

Seeding The Fish

Why did I suddenly think
of this today caught among
fishes in netting of our nerves
sharper, sharper spine
or skeleton
poisonous as you
told me later when we
wound each other a slight
premonition of ruin
knots no bigger than a tear
or drop of blood
it had broken off,
but what breaks off can still be felt
in rocks of the spine land belongs
to the past.

A NOTE FROM A FOREIGNER

This hypnotic apocalypse
surprised us then when
I reread as witness it was
love that contains loss
as premonition
trickling between
my blood rembrance
of past microscopic life
slide of champagne bubble
hum of finger
on rim of glass
or was it summers cicadas
These are invention,
weak composition
there is form in all things
revelation exists as this
tricking me into tying
secrets to myself.

A Simple Break Of Water

I remember
around eleven o'clock
courtyard with its fountain
that simple break of water
still and foreign chill
will always be ruin for me.
They passed your name
around the world twice
before anyone could notice
it was possible to witness
this with naked eyes
the precise moment
power gathers itself,
high inner court as hate
penetrates and pervades
preserves all it traps
before we can figure it out.

For Things Unnamed

Doing it for the first time
without plan like floating
a boat inside a bottle

sent no manual
or instruction to break this
patterning
begin by imagining
impossible
I need to tell him
pain can wipe out
all memory of pleasure
one gesture
is mistaken
for a lifeline
the first person
not to lie or create
lies that others draw on.
Red. Blue. True.
Inker of hell
look in his eyes
You can tell.

INTERROGATION

Under the blossoming almond tree,
the guillotine,
fate's rusted edge
dark stone presiding

We hold cold tight: despite white bulb glare
high inner court as power sharpens
human voice their
instrument of petrified heart.
I have never seen such
darkness in pith of human soul
What layers of hell did he crawl out of
to climb into the sound of his own voice?
I heard the voice last month, black stone
cast down
where a man died.

I was witness to stoning
I was witness to broken man
I felt him die in my arms
It was part of a plan.

Ars Poetica From
A Lover Proclaiming
To Be A Stranger

You brought me desire. I showed you
my hand in a fist. You opened my palm.
memory was there, it seems that feeling
lasted forever . A thousand touches I
cannot wash from my hands
our sex inking as honey
what touches you in hollows,
curves to follow stirs in moments,

when you embody me, for this
is the grace of remembered things, coming
from nowhere, spreading out over lips
thighs, as close as I am to you
bare, warm, skin-
all I desire of primal
things.

THE SLEEPERS

In a foreign landscape,
we are ghosts
entering the nights séance
capture what is still unaccounted
immigration beads, the flags of paper
still swathed in wax seal and twine
they speak to us through
documents and deeds
in the dust there are everlasting notes
you smell them on the old streets.

One explosion after another
to draw you out of existence
I show you
blood on my lip, but this dried quickly
resembles salt of memory and desire
you were my promise

lips that gave everything
as your mouth moving across my body
and warmth presiding over
second pilgrim of cold: enter dead land,
as they send mysterious chill.
Some you hide, others you hate you
use you until they change us
like gunpowder
the black, exists so you can taste it
just a bowl of burned rice
or was it the cave offering a place
in the stones
to sleep on the rough earth
pulling the ground around you
What does it mean to sleep
like a dog without a blanket.

ELLIS STREET

I am the room in a disused brothel,
the one left behind
on the blue wallpaper tiny reindeer orchids.
Women's voices
the ice means something
the crevice deep,
slipping against the womb
arms strong enough to hold us
when diamonds

split

apart

I am carving a garden of sapphire flowers,
the freesias same fragility .
Delicate. Everything thinks it might perish.
Ravaged gardens. I am in closer to the musk,
breathing perfume on a throat.
Leaves. Stamen. Amorous.
I am absorbing your shape and
all the vague moisture.
Skin.
Its silk links me to heat, adulterated
polished,
warm hands of a body,
in its arms, the mechanism is beautiful.

Sensual Math

When together I figure this sensual math
count every place we touch
everything before and after this
every reverie with whispered voices
under nights arcade like this one
I know nothing about the edge of love,
sharpened for how long the wild nights
the diminishing number of times
this dancing descent or the legend,
slowly dissolving in the white ground
of you, or anyone, but if they ask me,
I will tell them, what I figured out
the mechanism still beautiful.

ROOM

I came here expecting to find
distance between ourselves
who knows where to look
switching naked bulb, long night,
everything I remember, hotel, monastery
cell
saying hell to everything. Everyone.
For this was the blue room that took us in
edge of a blade, broken mirror
razor worn where luck intersects
this flat paper
soluble pile of hundred dollar bills
face of Jesus

when we look in this mirror
we can be anyone
king or whore what is more
or remote possibility
we can retrace our steps from heaven
to hell
make Dante laugh Orpheus
cry as well
who can pull your thought
through the eye of his needle
if he is right, I only need
to swallow one bullet
to be his angel.

Any one of these lies
may come true
it happens to be like memory
revision of thought
rewards you just to accept
your arm is soft around my neck.

Drowning Out All Human Sound

What ties me to you, especially in rain
when first rain is delicate,
as pure water poured
into pure water stays the same,
but suddenly it isn't delicate
there is a difference
in qualities
rainwater that has fallen
on a mouth of a mountain ridge,
gestures slowly
bowing down as it runs between rocks
like someone
who knows he is going to fall,
then turns into heavy waterfall,
drowning out all human sound
like glass splinters in a mouth.

An outpouring
makes everyone in the railway station hush.
Even the stray dogs look scared, waiting in
open doorways.
If anyone can break through this thick
silence
there will be a flood.
What we desire, wish for, what is forbidden
and desired.
Waiting for something that is not. Rain.
Sometimes there is no sound present to put
a limit on solitude.
Sheltering in a station with strangers, the
pregnant, the old and tired.
All the caress of a storm.
We interrupt solitude with our lives.

REQUIEM

For a long time
I cannot imagine,
the future falling out of itself
one broken thought
carries away whole dreams,
wedding flowers settling in minds
of survivors
and now also fortune tellers whispers
promises more before everything
was taken away, what comes out
of foreign cargo carries dreams.
Tell your lover wreckless
things
are beautiful

that a lover is desirable
witness
for she knows what you love
exotic and erotica
desire
this sexual enigma
enough to turn you into her legend.

In wounded space
I let your arm fall
across my heart.

Memory lives
inside us dies
water and a tomb
dreams chained
to timbre our soul.

Drawing Of Red

I was magi of night
burning red candles in every atrium
so they told you to possess me
all my life I loved you
so many times
possessed, dispossessed
enough to make me weep.
I was witness to your heart as it bled
and the way love's binding held us
the tissue weaves tight
so I cried for you
you who holds my dying within himself
I died with you as you were dying
death was a simple act of leaving
breath behind.

Drawing Of White

The ghosts are self-possessed
they fall dead at the edge of life
they enter this house and spy on us
then hide like children.
they refuse to speak to us
so I asked the saint to pray
for you if you would listen

I lit candles at the alters
In rooms of the naked
I was witness to the night
of missing things
loss reminds us
- I misheard you

so many times
but this was the broken
breath, the bad news
of the worst time that our
lives knew, the sad
thing is they did
not tell us how to live through
an ending and the
most distinctive
thing is that I can not
kill them for destructive
behavior or force
him to speak out of his
bone cold silence-
I kissed my ghost
it feels like snow.

Drawing On Water

I walk on Piha beach, my
eyes shut
but rain knows how to pass
my sealed eyes and I
can tell from the salt sting it's
again sand that engraves
my vision
and in my memory I am
thinking of west coast days
except it is black sand in
letter unfolded its ink
yellowed and I
I can see your
face beneath waves,
the water wakes,
pulling you down like a
dark shell absent from
earth.

INVENTORY
OF PLACES
TO DIE

In winter you gather newspapers
these turn into walls in your hand
I pull the roof over you, grasping tiles
where night intercedes with stars
& moon
also those rooms a city makes
angels in Moscow
in some rooms
there are pillows puffed feather
blankets in some crevasses
winter sheets
(I remember his bed
of well-ironed laundry
Its starchy ancestry
comes to me
white room

last house).
City, you give us many places
cathedral doorway
park bench
public restroom
railway station
at the fountain of ice angels
one more dying
as snow falling
her broken wings snapped.
Thirty below zero
made leaving easy
undetermined touch of feather
on corner of cheek
to be read in whiteout
vague feeling in dead cold
gathered in your arms
when you had everything
hold me
if you go before me
leave the door open with your shoe.

WORD SHADOWS

Of our dreams
you tell me to go
I leave
let go of your hand
I return holding this mirror
and it is a dream
beyond mercurial silvering
for outside
there were only patterns
of moon, night passion, six stars.
Some seemed to wait
although bright ones
in those days
were nothing but
shadows still full of light
in folds of mirror.
these were only images
door, painted wall, white ceiling
someone seems to live there
although when I returned
the man was leaving.
He did not see us, in our shattering.

Songs Of Night

Since Pilate hand
kills what I am
reminds you of lambs they slaughter
another snow
but full of ashes
when you
in act of that other killing
bring their flag inside
to burn its stars.

Both of us want to stay
in darkened rooms
faces blackened by smoke
loss opens her robe to succor us

pass around milk that tastes of ashes.

Of all that is speech there is no word of you.
Of all that is heard there is time
when all love ends.
We are bones,
words fall like rain on each of us.
Do we divide part of love from us.
My heart, my liver, my skull.
Shall these Bones live?
In cool day, tree split,
my wrist bone was dry. For I
will not honor virgin,
hold spear,
fall to hurt.
My guts,
string of my eye.
Dry dune, fruit of womb,
gourd,
cross on the hill,
still lake,
rooms we sleep in.

White in gown of bone,
life still in us. As I am.
Sing to wind,
bone, sand, torn whole,

cave near the door.
I do not hope for more
than you gave me.
Let word say,
land lay on us
wing broken will not fly.
But will fan air in vain.
Air is dry,
for us rose end to no end.

In this land we own no one.
At first light, turn of a face,
time
I see a shape in vapor of air.
bones fall and shake
and wake us.

In fetid air,
dark, dank, mouth woke in a smile.
Grin was tooth less,
bone dry, white,
fell out like stone.
A ghost of river mouth.

Age of shark,
skin of snake rolls at your feet.
fig fruit cast on rock

like a dial of day
that will pass for one more day.
slot in time
sad scene, flute song,
stops starts,
like hope in steps of our mind,
stops starts,
mouth blown,
like a fly in your web,
on stair light will fade,
steps will stop.
Fade.
Fade.
Crack bones open,
chalk rice,
white grain, falls like rain.
But speak the word.
Walk where I walk.
Speak what I dare to say.
Stay with me a while.
Do not walk on bone path.
Stones cut your feet.
Straw shoe will keep rain out.
Gone in white.
In blue.
The hue I gave you in kiss.
Talk ether of silence.

Who will move me when you go?
Who will find your bone.
As we walk hills are far, land is past.
We will not go back.
Hold my hand.
Kiss me one time.
Who made bone fall like rain on the path.
Who made wine, water, sand,
a touch of your hand
made stone cool,
bread warm, sea foam,
this time we own.

The year we walk on roads and do not
speak.
The night we close our eyes but do not
sleep.
One move in time where light
folds like a sheath that holds us
cloud of tears,
road bent down to find this lost word,
like paper lost then found.
If we read,
if we heard,
if bone fell like rain on the sea of us,
shone in dark like red eye of wolf
world a light shone;

on snow reflect white now rain land,
night time comes to us,
wake of sleep,
wake of dream,
and wake of a death and cry of a man.
Avoid veil, horn keg with dark gunshot, last
red rock.

If you can transcribe
summer heat
in wet syllables

around a mouth
it is like this

how you softened
human words to whisper
in the prison
of your lipstick
red mouth.
That's where you left, sweet taste.
Like peony flower of red
to transplant it
make it deep
and permanent
where you are
but it is not me you are kissing.
It is someone else.

Weight Of Kiss

A feeling of mouth breath,
I know nothing about
depth of stone heart
or scars from this kiss
both dissolve into taste of us

I could sense splinter of naked color
it is closeness
of your perfume that hems your bare neck
this obsession more than carnal flower
on a throat
when rice paper door opened
fall of your beautiful shoulder.
Its trees budding with lime.

Apocalypse
Metamorphous

She came out of apocalypse
blackened
bush, tree, sky on fire,
gray smoke like cooking
smoke curling upwards past
the river

smelling of wild fire
grass in her hair

then she looked into his face
legend of lips burns
a long kiss

dedicating fire to you
heat in my body
to you.

On both sides of the river
pohutukawa trees as far as
eyes could see; but there
were none of those red
stamen that betray summer,
the heat of the land
had burned each bloom
to blackened husk

smelling of wild fire
grass in her hair

I want to hold
you, as if he is asking her to dance
warm hands of the man
on her hips heat of his body
passing as human
warmth through her thin cotton
dress

I feel like we are on the other side
I want to say things to you
never said among living

there is not much time

I am filled with so much
serene sadness
almost pleasure,
I will not forget your face
the way you welcomed me
on the threshold
of the land of the dead.

He moved towards her
without another word
he kissed her.
No longer feel thirst.
No longer feel fear.
One thing she understood
separated from each other,
we will be
human dust, particles
rising from fires into blood sky
This is the metamorphous that waited.

DIVERS MEMORY

What torments me is my thirst
all has been eaten
all has been drunk
we have no water
wait until this evening.
I do not understand.
Translate loss, word for word
far from here,
tap, drips water,
river runs over
rocks, fall on soft green moss
wet first of all
in cool dark of silent thirst,
but it is not your thirst.

To make a man understand
I was dreaming about holding
handfuls of snow
the whiteness of the cold
breaking icicles from roof
and sucking
but there is a tap
above the tap is a card
water is dirty
we are dying of thirst,
I will drink if you to join me
take a mouthful spit it out,
water is tepid sweetish,
smell of swamp
tadpole spawn, fetid gutter
this is hell
today, in our time,
hell must be like this
tap drips, we cannot drink.
Wait for something, nothing happens
nothing continues to happen
time passes drop by drop.

EXILE

I think of you, how you leave
gilded cage with open door
in some prophetic sign of feathers
imagine you have freedom's
wings
a thousand laurel
branches for luck.

I saw fates secret art
beneath black line of ink
Its mystery is known in fortunes
cave
grotto where you opened
your hand to woman
palm lined with gold
light from oriental lanterns.

CHINA BEACH

For what is left after
they stole from you,
but ether of judgment,
prolonged echo
transports power
to kill sleep corrupt long
nights pain stabs through dreams
as man runs with familiar eyes
of a woman watching him
who
looking again sees
street fires, rice paper poem,
jar of peach wine,
a kiss to remind us,

of perfumes
musk incense burning

one songbird
sings in limewood cage
enter through shuttered doors
color of green.

What is found after she
took you here
where perfume river flows
to remind him
you left fate outside your plans
for oriental things.

To a stranger she gives wings,
like those of a bird
to fly away with him.

Peacocks fly through black space
eyes bright and lacquered
the night finds a way

the closure of the mouth
and the opening again
as if testing the ripeness
of something

nibbling at the pomegranate
fruit, the buds, the dream.

Bird flies among lime flowers
of all the greens fly too
it is the green of your eyes
that matches
exquisite silk.

In the bloom of dusk
we talked for an hour
sweet juice
in the silver chalice
liquid perfumes a mind
sends images to dream
and it seems, nothing wakes her.

The ether of grass, the flower fades:
because the spirit blooms upon it:
surely the people are grass.
There is still the sound of cicadas at dusk
and the fetid smell
in an underground well.

Already there are mimosa petals
gathering like ghosts in the gardens.

Not Like A Fig

Every angel is terrifying.
And so I float between you
and some fretwork found in our
frames,
but we forget to decipher,
forget to transcribe.
When the wind full of world space
gnaws at our faces,
for whom won't the night be there,
desired,
gently disappointing,
a hard rendezvous for each broken heart.
Not ghosts, not angels.
Primal, we are born apart,
the wires of our wings clipped
in an ancient pain
we can never fly.

FRAGMENTS
OF THE HUMAN
HEART : PART I

Covert eyes
film his footsteps
thieves on the road:
break into this house
steal intimacy like rubies.

They stole places I owned,
our palaces,
the lakes of my eyes,
the river between
the art of stealing so many things
belonging to us, stolen.

Without maps I fall across boarders,
how bruises come easy.
I search for viable
photographs of lovers,
obsolete passports.
searching for secrets
grateful for air.

When you left - I began to forget
the sound of your voice,
curves of your body fading
until I was looking back into silence.

You kissed me all those years ago,
what was it you wanted back then?

The knife cuts words into legal notes
and all fragments
personal confidential letters inside
they were small words and hard to believe
cut in small pieces as they were silent
but they were words as you
remember - and yet another summer
the fortune located
when they broke the vault
two million dollars and marriage certificate
destroyed by axe and vermin.

CABOCHON

Winter echoes, trapped
Fainting with cold,
Covert surveillance
Spy on our invisible cache
Someone shakes the future
Turns the compass beyond winter
Tears that fall
behind the sun
bury us in ashes.

FARMERS OF SORROW

First to the way human waste falls skyward
turns into rain clouds behind sky
no one noticed
the chaos in a room
we assumed was filled with treasure
until a sudden downpour threatens
to drown you
like a river drawing all
human thought
garbage floats into you.

See the last ridge of the city
before the river
from which you can never

interrupt the flow
same year
long tears sets the dateline
where the soul must have been.
The farmers of sorrow
they did not like flowers
they burned the trees
and changed the climate.

Defying the rules of birth's reward
small gain this falling rain on water
weaving the water into a palace
river as room
we are gone as a stone thrown in a river
it is dark in there.

Marcia

I heard of an airman
who fell from sky so beautifully
that some say that he was
silk falling on the grass
silence flowering on his
broken lips
that if she kisses him
a women would know his smile
as his only wound.

THE SUBJECT OF PILGRIMS

How we gathered our child
second pilgrim of cold: enter dead land,
as they send mysterious chill
our shelter stolen one morning
(stay outside) and I show you
blood on my lip, but this dried quickly
resembles salt of memory and desire
but you were my promise
lips that gave me everything
as your mouth moving across my body
and the warm presiding over.

FANSHAWE STREET

I know
That every promise is given
but who promised the woman
who sweeps up after war
only what happens after
subversive acts
the long silence, trading
what is left
after the losses,
blue ice orchid
given away for bread
or a book of poems
these remains of life, we keep.

ON THE TRAIN TO TOULOUSE

A man watches a woman – some secret
boundary of her skin
when she exposes the gap,
between her blue jeans - white shirt.
In this change of whiteness,
desire her - red silk
As if an impulse received from the archer
to find the core of heart inside this red
As if she tattooed her soul,
so he would find her,
when the sun has set,
when the moon has set,
and the last human fire has gone out,
he will find her,
shadow under this heart.

FEVER WIND

I was frightened. That is why
I left you in a hurry.

I thought I would rather
risk death from destruction
by some fever-wind,
or starvation, rather
than stay behind with you.

I will go first before
many of those who still have to leave,
I will go in the middle of many
who are now leaving. Look
back to how it was before
I left you,

look forward to how we
will be together.

There is a place
in the bleaching
of bones
where those who perish
in that place
and in places there are
signs of life departure
piles of sad bleached bones
unidentified
as man or animal
where men perish....
collected as souvenirs
by every passerby
and left in a heap
markers to show the way,
guide a road through the desert
for future travelers
on the pathway
traces
    of nothing,
it is not hard to convince me
this could be true.

WOMAN
AS YOU OBSERVE
HER

You smiled as I photograph
woman carrying a bundle
of dry sticks on her back
weighted down to earth with firewood
she carried angels and sticks
she walked alone where verdigris
grass hems the shores
of Lake Limone
her skin burning with the sun
how long between the citron and pond
and the scent of bruised lemon
wood is her perfume.

ABSINTHE

A woman hidden,
in dark of a camera,
waiting for a man to develop
her remaining images,
lips
to retouch her smile,
erase harsh lines caught
in fine aperture
film develops inside
how lines appear in a mirror,
this soft erasure of time.

Do you feel you were living
someone else's life
when life develops into
the same picture as his.

What can you see?
I see two souls as black
kicking against white edges.
It is not the way to travel
together
this black testimony.

CALENDAR OF FRAGILITY

The calendar of fragility
holds forty months
of tears and you, trusting
beyond every death
decoding feelings
you believe enemies fought
can be beaten
for all who are shattered by
their fragile excuses where
the wallet rules without humanity.
Fight on. At times lost in fog,
my fog, his fog, their fog.
Listen to local bell, its tongue peeling hard.
The weight of a soul being beaten,
feeling thin,
fragile and heavy.

A note of linden flower, white thorn &
burning wild grasses & the powdery velvet
wallflower
To have you in my room (documented)

each flower who sees the weeds growing
this certainty, the gorse by the mudflats,
dandelion dilated yellow, like an oracle in
grass
clover for sorrow, rue for fate, her hands
tied
each porcelain stalk
and you sheltered in the hothouse.
But know that every word exists. Amorous.

Carrying embers into my bones
the poet only believed
in relics of saints. Of heart.
Until I felt the pulse between
all its flame at the base of a throat
this wild grass exposes itself
in our carnal meadow
every summer extinguishes itself
sphagnum fur and moss
lilacs in the yard, French roses in a jar,
to undo wisteria on your iron gate, their
branches
unlock.
Every weed is incendiary
I have a match. No lighter.

THE SLEEPWALKER

A man is walking barefoot
Carrying a feather pillow
Under his arm
Walking a concrete cliff edge
Alone and in the dark
A canvas bag on his back
Heavy with mistakes
Night is black hemp blindfold
Slip knot tied way too tight
Weights down on his eyelids
Sleep walking far from his bed
Two dents in a feather pillow
Two sheets crumpled
A long trail of broken shells
A man sees and hears nothing
No one could read your warning
We were fish caught inside dreams
Ghost palms broken by passing hurricane
Sleepers awake on the inside
Inside another sleep
We wake again.

An Observation Without Seeing

Now that my road is yours
its unlimited length
of dust
the blinding plans of night
to keep your eyes from my face
old stones, blue fires of fate
the exact moment
hypnotized. I have absorbed
the tender hungry core
and what is more of you
I have already described
the muscle and bone of
raw feeling
the reason I undress
in a hurry and cannot leave
this Lover
love of the old love
the blinding arras
stitched with sand and dust
saying yes

and the filigree of night
held the ancient coin
the blackened one
they tossed back
and it lands on the road
the face looking up
saying yes
lead me to your body
by the branch from a tree
the warm interior
the same as the night
all silver bells
my sight is yours.

PLACES FOR LEAVING

When a rock cracks is no longer a rock
but broken for time.
I will join you in the fissures, between seams
of rock and fish, our bone story.
Questions are this. Who was snapper.
Who is saint fish.The dory.
It is pure whiteness , no longer fossil. It is
not relic
but a mistake of whiteness. It is part of after.
And now.
In the weight of waves when all seems
drowned together.
Lover. You follow behind tangle me up in a
seaweed rope.
Even an uneven knot of marine lettuce and
kelp. Help
keep her balance, this shift of driftwood.
Inside a floating bottle. Small piece of paper
with directions back here. Decisions like lies
suddenly changed. I am no map maker. But I
found myself leaving you as I lost my way.

INVENTORY

There was more to tell him.
Witness as limited as time made
shadows and bruises extravagant
like elegant medusas
where roses appear between animal
and
dark bruises almost
deep blue, like marks that find themselves
later a fist
beating on the drum, her ribs.
How did this happen so suddenly.

Eulogy For A Lover

Where I shall return in the end
the river into the depth of the ocean
the water, so clear almost
sage green
dark circles under the shores of your eyes
the river to ocean, his blue lips.
How did this happen so suddenly.

After the drowning
green ocean fish swimming further than
water
and with him is caviar
black glistening seeds bursting apart
I have tasted them in a mouth

sex of adulterated night
beats rhythm, ornate mast, incendiary
primordial night
its lasting secret keeps coming back
each clasp mounted horizontally
changes to fire, make tissues gasp
because you love a single
button touched and polished
with his fingers.

JOURNEY

Following her ghost. A dream as it was
perfect
a ruin of painted fence
lichen white wood
tiny cemetery flowers
I felt the dead in the cold
and there is still color in it
after the taro and broken shell
black pearls of her necklace
the vague smell of damp wood smolders
comes as a ghost on the same hill
the fall of her shoulder
where he kissed her.

Outside Warm Rain Falls

Carry all the tears of women
Into the water
When she will see
Looking deeper into equal waves
These should be returned
Before they mark the tides
With surface prayer.

Stone Fruit

In each room of the house
Leave bowls of plums
Dusted with stories of the road
To Compostela
I am going to live
On those plums.

Bones And Dream

The palace where he returns in the end.
Water can reflect in his eyes. Tears are no
answer.
What he wanted at the approach of a mouth.
Let the river enter
an arrangement of water
following the painted wave
transplanted from one ocean of salt.
What is left on his skin.
What is allowed after the cold pacific, water
knows, land knows, everything
floating, this broken cargo to keep the lice
from our skin, drowning
from our bodies, to feel your arm around my
shoulder, your lips
for the last time.

THUY'S ROOM

The room where she returns in the end
The imprint of his head left on a pillow
Dying was colder than he imagined
The life melting
And inside him is cold bone.
I have picked flowers with no perfume
Danced alone in a palace room
I have watched you kiss a woman there
A childbearing woman with long dark hair.
I have felt the dead in the cold of linen
I have laid down where his body has been.
Am I the one to stitch the tears
Or weave each past night,
each coming night into a clean sheet
laced with nightshade
to use on another bed.

And In The Morning
(Invitation to Wake)

Open the shutters
Open the doors
And outside the three caged
Peacocks and a thousand eerie calls
From the old quarter
Citadel extreme oriental
And the axe fell two thousand times
Where the garden was red blood
Frangipani trees, grow the
Blossoms bruise by falling
The harvest designated by hand
The hand held by you
As the peacock song warns us
I guessed at what was happening.

ONE POEM

A thousand kilometers from here
Out through the red delta
Lines of sight
Until stone steps
And empty rice silos
Inventory notes in each
Tin can
Then sealed glass jars with wax
I shoved the dirt
It filled with water
Notice when
There was nothing left to drink.

IDENTITY

I wondered how long it would last
The tricolor rag
Five pointed star
We begin to scratch a mark
Noughts and crosses
Wasting our saliva playing games
On the concrete wall
When the rice was gone
The briefcase emptied
Bright red flag
One bloody sheet
One dirty blanket
The mattress still warm when we left.
Two steps forward
Two steps back
When monkey cages were smaller.

THE ANALECTS X11.1

Confucius Temple has two roofs, yin and
yang,
a chinoiserie of flying eaves and clay tiles.
Dragons decorate the beams with power and
fortune
but the bodies are placed so that the entire
beast cannot
be seen.
Dragons must not be shown in their entirety,
Dragons must not be shown
Dragons must not be
Dragons must not
Dragons must
they must always disappear into words or
water.
In smoky shadows of temple eaves, relics of

Ghost,
its chill bones digging
up umbilicus & abacus of
Confucius's words...
do not look unless it is in accordance with
the rites;
do not listen unless it is in accordance with
the rites;
do not speak unless it is in accordance with
the rites;
do not move unless it is in accordance with
the rites.

THE LAST CIRCLE

It was beautiful silver filigree
Despite the opium inside
Along its embroidered shaft
The flame of a lamp
I bent to kiss him
Lips of warm escape route
Where saliva is collected
And drops were buried
Evaporate and I wait
To touch this sacrament
Dark dragon
Burning
After the all night flame
Narcotic sleep.

HOTEL SEQUENCE

Clutching a piece of white paper
and printed poster
still no curfew at night
as men
search her body for jewels and weapons
secret and locked.

Through the bars thinness
fingers pinching ribs carved
through her shirt
what she left as rags
to inherit her fabric
its sin and error
the lonely compartment
what is taken from her
attached and stitched
fabric of this entry

and flowering between us
desire and design
of the past and future.
We are blood
but what is the ending
we dreamed in blood beginning
filled with blood that never heals
red flowers enter
returning to my hands
the petals have silk and velvet odor
and they feel warm with dreams
disturbing the dust on a bowl of stars
for you to open the shutters
and put the flowers in a glass jar
green stem in a slice of water
the night smells red roses again.

OF BLUE

Here the street signs. Now the traders names
painted out, leaving the pale green
shutters of windows, closed in the after-
noon,
where an artist presses his brush against
blank paper
the brush from the water then the dark
pressing finds
the ink is absorbed, by white paper.
of initials carved into the first world
of the woman and the silent paper
her shadow is yours.
If you have come back to me
blue signs like an island for the poets
the other was more than a scar in my flesh
only the initials.

WATER SEQUENCE

I do not know how things vanish
after we inhabit the water
you move like a swimmer
I remember this served its purpose
beautiful as it was before
our faces become faded
because one became too much like
the other
until they could not wrench us apart
this is the use of memory
which can never heal the dream.

And the water stretched both arms
to hold us

you became my ocean
because one became too much like
the other
until they could not find us apart
we float, the blue around us,
marooned like a boat
we float, buoyant with dreams
our arms are the sea
last artist
last poet
and you become my escape
this freedom like driftwood
the night still smells of salt.

You become my lover
that I may touch your skin
and the king called in
as my soul
begins to fall
it was all that I had
to keep this heart unbroken
so they deliver impotent rage
the hand is a Lord over women
and the beast rich in rage
or rags or of trespass
kicked each bone
to release a bruised odor

unmending, or bending
let him be violent
first snap the strings
with his knife from its leather
where a man might slice the cover
in order to
tear apart the book
of this secret as it is locked, or unlocked
under the dead leaves
I imagine you
sorting and counting only unending pages
the deception in this origami
I am afraid you must cut it
for dark hearted roses
are folded into another pattern.

Of all things done, or dented
He said, I have done and said in order to
speak,
or be spoken
to speak like ink talks
to tell you to leave
through the door we never opened,
so we returned to dance the waves
inhabit an ocean, like a shell
filled with sand
we are water and dream of water.

Garden In Indochine

Through the gate, which has always been
there
And the path towards the door, which has
always been
Unlocked
As if it has seen, the bird in bamboo cage
Fly mesh in the shutters.
As if you unheard footsteps hidden in room
Had the book of sutra naked as you were
Opened by fingers wet from her
As if you were coupled
And you, lover?
We moved and they changed their position
And pulled the sheet over

As the pages turned
To look down into the fish pool
Silk grass and emeralds in the mud
And the fish swam quietly
The swim in the drift of night
As the pool was completely moonlight
And the pink lotus flowers in front of us
Push aside night
The leaves were filled with pearls
Deep in the mattress mantra we move
Fingers and vulva
Became heat in the heat
And women are figured in ink
The look that is looked after
The names of lovers
There are dreams out there
Smell her jasmine
And she is no virgin
Below the rich circulation of glistening eggs
A woman sorting their sticky pattern
and counting her children.

EVE

A woman's voice from long ago
Fair with an accent of white feathers
I had forgotten her sound
She whispered from above
"it is all about love,
                it is only about love,
                it's just you don't see it yet"
Tell them we're ready as a Man and Woman.
We fall down instead of upwards
Like the angels
Climbing down from the mountainside
We are gardeners
Ancient dirt embedded
Under our nails

In the dissolving ghost's find each other
Following footprints as they disappear
At the earth's edge
I know you as a ghost
I know your words
In the garden
You must be very silent
She is counting the years lost
Like leaves on a deciduous tree
Tracings of her
As she remembers
Looking for you in
A stone jar of dreams
Tear open the moon
The fragrance of musk
A paper shadow on the bedroom wall
All are censored by Saints
From inside
They turn the sky deep red at sunset
Your breath cool on my face
Feels like autumn hymn
What do we give away to become
Pilgrims and hermits in a cave in Corinth?
What would I give to see you again?

Translated
From Valentinio

All I see is the essence of us, immediately
In the signature
Horoscope, riddles, shuffled King

I saw the lover and the loved
In tea leaves
And cartography of the palm.

One does not teach the other this.

It is of this truth that the other speaks
Aflame or ablaze and by this love
Which belongs to us

Something more, she said
While nights are dreams

Of things unknown, that leads us
To more
And do not think
At the time (after)

I fully realized
You can receive this

Husk of meaning around everything
Watching the furrow widen behind you

Observer and observed
To report the fire and ash
The singeing of dreams

As you seduced another to love
Then the mystery was accomplished

In every movement
And whose body
Stands as a shrine
Illuminated by the diffusion of light
Perfected by love

Impregnated with memory, I was here.

Of all we know, nothing would be
Unknown.
Pray.
You did not see the boat
Returning to those who reach
Out for them.

Pray for water
perpetual
to do with fish

And also pray for this dream
The touch of an eyelid closing
This could not have been seen before.

Essays

What began as studies, of the female mito-chondria DNA, the information continues and in determining the content: missed clues. A woman, her womb grows out of the emptiness of its shape. For it is said that we descend from just seven women. In knowing this, he sees her for the first time.

There was symmetry in walking barefoot. Simply by losing our shoes we shall find it. And we end up in the same place. A few leaves jangling in their intactness with tiny rust holes costing a few letters. Burning wild grasses & wallflower brushed on the walls and you in my room. Your kiss was a flame, on my lips carried by physical incantation, surrendering through endless warmth, to make my blood burn and flow with your saliva as sweet warm lava, every release, unreal. The rhyme is also yours to enter the palace of body of love, knowing the secret, the nights, mornings, afternoons, I discover a lifelong taste for this divine recipe, this nectar entering my mouth, liquid languish of the ancient, slipping your tongue into the closest part, knowing the secret feel of you, I need no longer dream it. Blindfolded destinies. There are no other guests in the villa except my lover and me.

She makes him forget there was a night in which he was ever asleep.

Periodic Table

Woman: All we call swimming is sacred history. All we call walking is sacred history....they are principal events in chronology. What does walking or swimming prove? That there is weight to all we call water.

Written in water, enameled in blue, make the study of seas; its existence makes a rich world, she listens to diamond waves that wet her bare feet. One piece of water cut for a lake; one for her drinking glass. When she drinks she became animal, animal rests in the fountain of the possible, soul make her body, and his body floats, as her body walks, who is invited into science of real.

Who can drink water without in some way becoming water. Who can show me what can be? Often I drown, then who will carry me into clouds, from cloud to cloud, until rains falls, as I fall, a novice who does not know which way to heaven, and my words are merely lent to you, I will watch truth, as skill, how he swims like a flying fish, from sky or water but water this man inhabits is her also. When the sea was searched land was found for us, in shadows of real things.

A woman must solve her own riddle. This hypnotic apocalypse I reread as witness it was bodies cleaved velvet to one other, when body silk warmed all night on his mattress, when there was delicious fever, stars were poem, their voices were passing moans drifting into a palm to psalm; the gilt edge, vellum and morocco, until books come down, death Psalm 23 chosen from a hundred plowed fields, creates two lost pilgrims at the harvest wedding in the small church cloudless day, golden bands cast and shiny, but unlucky authors to fate, as it publishes itself, it shows in the direction of stream of unconsciousness, when you are carried by pallbearers and unaware the stream truly is blood, every drop alive, truth does not contain sensitivities, all things are its organs, dust and stones, vague errors and lies contain loss as premonition trickling between my blood remembrance.

I know nothing about the edge of love, sharpened for how long the wild nights beat, the diminishing number of times this dancing descent finding fragile knots line upon line lineament of legend, slowly leaking their ghosts in the white ground. Of you, or anyone, but if they ask me, I will tell them, as personal allusions what I figured out, such mechanism is beautiful.

Thoughts deliver us to memories, like a string of beads which shut us in a jail of glass. We need a change of objects. For all this I asked you by its promises of heat between rains of you between slats of moisture. I had taken my place above your open mouth. A tongue cannot be tamed. This revelation exists, tricking me into tying secrets to myself. How long is this rope of infinity. But what do you think, to brand my lips so that I may breathe close. For a woman is laid down, as though green grass has been planted in an open field. The morning when gentle color comes back as though nothing happened.

She became a gardener, figs become grapes while she eats them, as her ghost confirms truths, they blossomed in her hands, they enter and disappear, divide and multiply like bulbs did once, as dirt on her hands comes by earth a hundred millions of miles deep, so flowering us to dream, as a body depends on the equilibrium of nature, seeds Prometheus Vinctus, as every lover is a divinity in disguise, heaven sent some insane angels, instructed by night and night explained the stars away, every dream was a dream in another woman's mind, that fastens these images hung as signs of our secret experience, and if they grope for it with fingers in tombs and sad broken angels, torsos of ruined houses, make tragedies and statues, if they steal our bed, in a conscious act, infinite lie stretched in a wide smile, we will do nothing, our hands glued to our sides, but in reading the apostles creed before sleep, stars and waves, feel closer, silver and blue as if two met and run into each others sleep under cover in this garden with so many flowers and wild ornaments.

I am the room in a disused brothel, left behind. On the blue wallpaper tiny reindeer orchids. Women's voices and the ice means something the crevice deep, slipping against the womb. Arms strong enough to hold us when diamonds Split apart. I am carving a garden of sapphire flowers, the freesias same fragility. Delicate. Everything that thinks it might perish. Ravaged gardens. I am in closer to the musk, breathing perfume on a throat. Leaves. Stamen. Amorous. The true garden is the gardener. I am absorbing your shape and all the vague moisture. I apply myself to the tendrils of reproduction. I put myself into the first temple, by its processions, as every tint in the secreting whole woman in infinite diameters.

All seems to wait, as if the genii of the body is fastened far back in the womb of things. Its silk links through genera soft and fluid. Parting from rudiments, into precise form before it, outline is changed together, adulterated polished and never the same. He casts warm hands under a body, as it is prepared by nature, reproduced in its buds, its ferns, its fir, its fur, with vegetable biography deep and sublime, lotus and palm, converts all things to its own ends, in its arms, the mechanism is beautiful.

She became a tent for a night. A thousand nights since then, passing the loss of everything. A sleep within a sleep. Some private dream. No longer a tenant or boarder, no longer know the times, politics, law of this place, or care opinions, customs and swords, universal hours, this man-ifold and duplex life arranged in recited money exchange, as living ends in funeral flutes.

Life dissipates to shadowy ether. No fences,

no rope, no string can hold us here. As a ghost once told her: It is all about love, it is only about love.... it's just that you don't know it yet. But even at the brink of sleep, at the boundary of life and angles of truth, we are dying. I have watched alone, in a belief that one could understand another, but flesh and bone are rivers and mountains separating people into distinct and lonely regions.

What if you come near to it, you are as remote, when you are near, as you are when you are farthest, the Ghost said, every thought is a prison. Then I love only the Poet, as they unlock the chains and bring us books. Ascend to truth, every sentence; each verse possessing truth will take care of its own mortality. I found within another world, a nest of worlds, the muse as a landlord and keeper, day and night are transparent boundaries and you can walk the world over, into celestial space, where stars divide so it does not stop. The Poet did not stop at the silver paper but read the meaning, and the paper she screwed up, put the world like a ball, in her hands. Writing of days, of wind and rain, waves that tilt the heavens, waterfalls of a thousand crashing streams, sights of hunger and cold, the stagnant waters of a writers mind.

Attached to the letter were two poems, as external conditions change, the soul changes as well, white in gown of bone, life still in us. As I am. Weakness follows weaknesses, thousands upon thousands of them. Sing to wind, bone.

sand, torn whole, cave near the door. I do not hope for more than you gave me. The Poet did not stop at the obituaries but read the meaning, and the names she read, put the words like soil, in her hands. In the dark citadel of the heart I know you. But the stars secretly engraved themselves on all four corners of my mind, a hundred million lights connecting unclear words. A heart adrift since the day of birth. And in your eyes, I see images of an endless string of nights and the future a series of graves not yet filled.

The present is also the silent burial of the green days, fresh leaves beginning to change hue, weaving in the shroud that covers our souls, I stare at the countless leaves in silence, the dark shadows under your eyes are familiar. Strange patterns on the face of an old woman. Since when did I become old? And might those tears of a woman contain my own tears as well? Words fall like rain on each of us. They fell vaguely, from the immensity of memory. Written in water, enameled in blue, make the study of tears; its existence makes the woman. All that we call woman is sacred history....tears are principal events in chronology.

THE CONTENT OF WATER

In the dark citadel of the heart I know you. And in your sad eyes, I see images of an endless string of nights and the future a series of graves not yet filled. And the present is also the silent burial of the green days, fresh leaves beginning to change hue, weaving in the shroud that covers our souls, I stare at the countless leaves in silence, the dark shadows from rows of tall bamboo are familiar. Strange patterns on the face of an old woman. I stare at the countless leaves; a crying woman lays her bare heart. Since when did I become old? And might those tears of a woman contain my own tears as well? (Tears) jade of sorrow, still intact, unmelted. They fell vaguely, from the immensity of memory. I have watched alone, in a belief that one could understand another, but flesh and bone are rivers and mountains separating people into distinct and lonely regions.

(Fade to bJlack).

Night. But the stars secretly engraved themselves on all four corners of my mind, a hundred million lights connecting unclear words. A heart adrift since the day of birth. Here are feet marked by a thousand scars, punctured by thorns of life. Here are hands, calloused and crooked, reaching out for a green dollar. These bones contain a soul but termites burrow into the house. I turn with my head bowed. Who wanders lost through one existence. Weakness follows weaknesses, thousands upon thousands of them. Tomorrows footsteps will accumulate upon the footprints of today. Don't be angry with us, these shriveled forms beg for money, these heavy bodies sunk too low, don't be angry with us who lost paradise. If you only knew how many times we panicked.

Wet raincoats and the sound of a city coughing as the locals share colds. Some women speak of a Jade Queen of the Immortals. Illness and misfortune falls on a woman who does not feel something deeper, the natural balance violated but gravity or moonlight restore the balance. The Jade Queen said, semen is closest to source and he believes her. Marry a boy for rice and silk. Even in hunger and rags one still knows shame. If you love me loan me cloth or loan me rice. It was just a look in passing. Had they not known each other well they might have passed by unknown. (There still are corners to the eyes).

You chanted prayers of salvation from over three hundred books. What good are all those characters? You get milk in the morning, rice at night. Enough bread. Enough. More than enough. He came to say: Leave me alone to live my own life. I am tired of this (repetition).

He cast off his disguise, which had produced no poetry. And returned to the coat he had put away, and his white cloth and shoes. And his shirt all faded blue from sunshine and dew. Intoxicated in a garden nameless and eternal. And he went away in search of two sides of a leaf or a blade of grass. To be a poet is to be lulled by the wind. To follow the moon in dreams and drift with the clouds. To let the soul be bound by a thousand strands. I am but a splinter because of a hundred precious loves.

The weather changes at the end of winter. The first colors in the city are green leaves with pink paper petals. Women pedal branches of peach blossom in from the countryside. If the beginning of spring seizes possession of its own privacy. Each unopened bud is a tiny needle. And the sun is ten thousand magnets.

The air is tinged with charcoal dust from outdoor cooking fires. In January and February, smoky shadows and the slow incense smoke. One moment the spare bed empty with cold indifference. Next a moment shared under a blanket, only to wake in a malarial sweat. Summer comes. She arrives with days long and damp. A crush of traffic noise heightened by the 40 degree heat, it floods the senses and disorientates.

The street outside is a tunnel of tamarind and mahogany trees festooned with power cables, like jungle creepers, colonial villas, balconied and shuttered, historical keepsakes behind flowers & fruited filigree, the padlocked iron gates.

It is said a woman is like a flower that has been brought out into a fresh bright place. Breathing in the free air of nature she is able to grow fragrant. Smothered with flowers on bodies of jade with fortunes read in three deep furrows on workers hands. Make rice wine from rhymes and verses from grenades. To have purpose and fire. Mother to thousands of lost destinies, to millions of children who wander naked and hungry over the earth. They said all suffering is this traced back to our own hearts.

Between four walls of air. Before someone looks down on me and thinks I am sleeping. Listen to the vespers. I whisper. The traces day by day fade with the grave marker. I am still afraid of an ending. I fall to the ground with clean hands.

The red sun touches clay tile roofs in every evening a syrupy light ripens the melon and cantaloupe painted colonial buildings. Late at night, outside in the alley, the men sleep. They sleep under white mosquito nets; bed as simple as bamboo mats rolled out on wooden tables. The wide boulevards are empty except for a few cyclos and a beer-stand dimly lit with a ten watt econ bulb. Then her black dog with his crooked smile.

Star jasmine perfumes the late night air. In the brief hours after midnight, the street is almost silent but at four in the morning, a rooster breaks sleep. Soon the women downstairs, will be tapping charcoal from yesterday's brazier, then the odor of chili and limes, burned offering, singeing of pig trotter over charcoal, dark fermented fish sauce, jasmine and cilantro, vine-weed, garlic, warm bread and roasted dog.

I gave you an offering. I would like to give you many more things but that's enough. I told you to sleep, Shhh.

Do not look unless it is accordance with the rites;

Do not listen unless it is accordance with the rites;

Do not speak unless it is accordance with the rites;

Do not move unless it is in accordance with the rites.

In the Temple garden, interactions with actual conditions; it is no more complete in itself than is a woman's pot of lime tea. Six or seven cups of tea while reading some lines from the Poet. Writing grief of days, of wind and rain, waves that tilt the heavens, waterfalls of a thousand crashing streams, sights of hunger and cold, the stagnant waters of a writers mind. Attached to the letter were two poems, as external conditions change, the soul changes as well, the Confucians chant until flowers wilt, seeds pass life in a clump of water.   (Fade to green)

The way of heaven is not all remote, they tell us. Wash a human heart and out it comes. One had to be taught, duties to oneself are not obligations. Confucius and Mencius were all guilty of overestimating the innate goodness of man, (please: no mention of face or reputation) but ones actions in life may be compared to tossing pebbles in a pond. Looking into the Well of Clarity, looking through a seam of ancient jade, no sooner has a stone fallen into water; it transforms into a small circle which becomes a larger circle. No one lives in isolation. The circle continues to expand until it covers the entire pond. There are ghosts throwing stones. Ghosts watching.

I have arrived back from the cold river of nihility. Kill those words of a poem that spring from far down in the throat. Seek no more fresh flowers, myriad lake, nor sounds of jade, my friend that sadness buried at the base of the soul remains untold. Our lives now lie within the sphere of "I". Having lost breadth, I seek depth. But the deeper I go, the colder I get.

Midnight in the Garden of the Temple of Literature

For Poet Do Trung Lai

Confucius Temple has two roofs, Yin and Yang, a chinoisereie of flying eaves and clay tiles. Dragons decorate the beams with power and fortune. But the bodies are placed so that the entire beast cannot be seen. When the temple was searched, poems were found for us, in the shadows of real things.

Under a hundred red lanterns, we collect documentation of the dreaming consciousness. I hold Five Lakes in Bac Minh Province in my hands. The lake which is most erotic. Your poem, Do Trung Lai. Translations of the old wind but in the image born of my breath. Like the Tam legend who has come to Eau river. Wash a Poet heart and out it comes.

I read your river poem from the center. At the heart of the circle. For ones actions in life may be compared to tossing stones in a pond. Looking into the Well of Clarity in the Temple Garden, seeing through a seam of ancient jade. No sooner has a pebble fallen into water; it transforms into a small circle which becomes a larger circle. No one lives in isolation. The circle continues to expand until it covers the entire pond. There are ghosts throwing stones. Ghosts listening. When some-one is reading and their voice becomes drowsy. Turning vegetables into mint. The silent burial of words as soon as I speak.

Bamboo boats turn into dragon boats. River water turns into dragon wine of a thousand years. If translators are architects of image, do I use the force of vocabulary, not simplify, one lake to sink love- sickness. Do I soften edges to a kiss as I read a lake of water red, like lipstick. Shall I bar trans-lation of valuable texts. Tear them up so that you can clean your feet. An ink stone with such a hard surface, that the stick glides over it, without leav-ing any deposit of ink

That river has only one colour. Who can read your poem without in some way becoming the river? What does translation prove? Your words are merely lent to me. No wall, no rope, no string can hold your words here. Tomorrow when all Poets disappear... we that have read poems in the belief that we could understand each other. But flesh and bone are rivers that separate us into distinct and lonely regions. If one lifts the door a little while leaving, there is no sound. It is sad to think that our words, indifferent to our leaving, should remain unspoken after we have gone.

Shall we cast off disguises that produce no poetry. Return to the coats we put away and a lake to wash the four part traditional shirt, to wash the headband, to wash the back silk pants.

As I thin the pages left behind, I catch the faint scent of lotus, which seems quite occidental. Do Trung Lai's shirt all faded blue from sunshine and dew. Intoxicated in a garden nameless and eternal. The way he goes away in search of two sides of a leaf or a blade of grass. Please wash them in one separate lake.

The French call this the cloud that hangs between rain and fog: crachin, or a "spitting rain". This makes a distinction between the summer monsoon. The rain that sits in your own heart. If it were written who would I give it to? Silence. The silence is an acceptance of fault. Question. From your mouth no word of appreciation, no argument or criticism, no answer to my question, from beginning to end all that comes out of your mouth is a laugh. (Who wouldn't grow angry)?

The nights have been like this, we sleep side by side. Each morning sharing all, a bowl of rice, a cup of tap water sweet with arsenic. Each cup reminds me. Poison tastes like honey.

(Fade to black).

(F R A G M E N T S)

Dust, ashes, sand. Gritty boundaries can be read like elegant text. The paper flaw touching the final line, reads: *To be grateful for fragments leftover. The remains.*

S U S A N   B L A N S H A R D

Susan Blanshard was born in Hampshire, England. She is an internationally acclaimed poet, essayist, literary editor, and author of more than 34 books. Selected poetry and essays are published in *The World's Literary Magazine, Projected Letters, Six Bricks Press, Arabesque Magazine, Lotus International Women's Magazine,* ICORN International *Cities of Refuge.* PEN International *Women Writers' Magazine.* PEN International Writers Committee *The Fourth Anthology, Our Voice, Nuestra Voz, Notre Voix.* Her literary essays *The Pillow Book, Four Recipes, The Traveler, Orientation,* published in *Arts And Culture, Lotus International Magazine,* Hanoi. Her collected poems *Running the Deserts, Midnight Mojave* were included in the Vaani *9.69 seconds,* a collection of short stories and poems dedicated to the London Olympics 2012. She has published book-length poetic prose: *Sheetstone: Memoir for a*

Lover, Sleeping with the Artist, Memoir of Love and Art: Honey in My Blood. Susan is married to an artist and author. They have two adult children.

www.ingramcontent.com/pod-product-compliance
Lightning Source LLC
Chambersburg PA
CBHW031305060726
47590CB00003B/1067